WARRIOR QUEEN

Jim Eldridge

Illustrated by **Patrick Miller**

In my long career as a writer I have written 100 books, 250 TV scripts and 250 radio scripts. My favourite topic is history, especially the Ancient Romans and the Ancient Britons (the Celts). Both of these came together with the Roman invasion of Britain in 43 CE.

By 60 CE most of England and Wales was under Roman control, with sporadic uprisings by the Britons. Then, in 61 CE, came the biggest rebellion of all. It was led by Queen Boudicca of the Iceni tribe. After Boudicca's rebel army defeated the Romans at Colchester, Britons from other tribes flocked to join her.

This story, *Warrior Queen*, is told through the eyes of two young people – Aithne, a twelve-year-old Briton, and a Wise Woman; and a twelve-year-old boy called Castus, half-Roman, half-Briton – who get caught up in the rebellion from opposite sides.

I do hope you enjoy it.

Jim Eldridge

A MAP OF BRITANNIA
FROM THE TIME OF
QUEEN BOUDICCA

MONA (ANGLESEY)

MENAI STRAIT

THE GREAT ROAD /
WATLING STREET

CAMULODONUM
(COLCHESTER)

VERULAMIUM
(ST ALBANS)

LONDINIUM
(LONDON)

3

Cast of Characters

Aithne
(*say* Ethnee)
Twelve years old
A girl from the Iceni tribe and a
Wise Woman

Drustan
Aithne's father
A warrior of the Iceni tribe

Castus / Caradoc
Twelve years old
A servant in the Roman army

Queen Boudicca
(*say* Boo-dicca)
Leader of the Iceni tribe

Suetonius Paulinus
(*say* Sway-tony-us Paul-i-nus)
The Roman Governor of Britannia

Nova
Eighteen years old
A Wise Woman of the Iceni tribe

Urien
A British rebel warrior chief
from the Silures tribe

Garth and Trey
Warriors of the Iceni tribe
Friends of Drustan

Chapter 1
The Island of Mona

Britannia, 61 CE

Aithne stood at the water's edge, looking towards the mainland, from this point just a mile away across the Menai Strait. She could see the Roman fort, with its walls made of wooden stakes and piled turf, and the observation towers at each corner.

We are watching them, and they are watching us, she thought.

Flags and banners fluttered over the fort, each bearing a different symbol for the different troops: here a bear was depicted, there a stork, and above them all, the eagle – the symbol of Rome and its power.

She heard a movement beside her, and knew from his footfall and his familiar smell that her father, Drustan, warrior chief of the Iceni, had joined her.

'You look worried, little one.'

Aithne bridled at this. She was not a 'little one', she was twelve years old and already considered a Wise Woman because of her power of second sight. Not that it really was second sight, she admitted to herself. It came from watching. The way people moved. The way they spoke. The looks they exchanged. What their hearts felt.

Her father sighed as he saw the look of annoyance on her face.

'My apologies, grown-up one,' he said.

Aithne relented immediately. She turned to her father and wrapped her arms around him.

'I'm the one who's sorry, Father. I shouldn't have been upset. I know you only call me that when you're worried about me.'

'I'm worried about everyone on this island,' admitted Drustan. 'We're all that remains of the rebellion against the Romans.'

Aithne knew this was true. Nearly everyone on the island had fled here to escape from the Roman advance across the country. There were about a thousand people on the island, many of them warriors, but a great number were Druids and Wise Women, or women and children. Across the narrow Strait, the Roman army was said to be five thousand strong.

'I fear the consequences if the Romans take us by surprise,' muttered Drustan unhappily, 'but we will fight to the last.'

Suddenly they heard shouting and turned to see two men running towards them.

'A body!' shouted one. 'We've found a body!'

* * *

A boy had been washed up by the sea and lay face down on the pebbly beach. He wore just a loincloth, and as

Aithne and her father drew near they could see that his back was criss-crossed with livid wheals.

'He's been whipped,' said the elder of the two men.

Drustan kneeled down beside the body and put his fingers against the boy's neck.

'There is a pulse,' he said. 'It's faint, but he's alive.' He stood up. 'We'll carry him to our house. Aithne, see if your Wise Woman skills can revive him.'

Aithne followed her father and the two men as they carried the limp body of the unconscious boy. Aithne's hut, like all the others, was made of skins draped over a frame of long wooden branches.

Inside the hut, the men laid the unconscious boy face down on a bed of animal skins.

'He must have come from the mainland,' said the other, younger man. He scowled. 'He must be Roman.'

'He looks like a Briton,' countered Drustan.

'He may look like a Briton but he smells Roman,' the younger man insisted. He opened the boy's mouth and smelled his breath, then turned to them, a look of triumph on his face.

'Their breath smells different because of that food they eat. Snails and such. I can smell it on him. He's Roman! The Council must be told!'

'I'm sure they are aware of his arrival already,' said Drustan. 'Enough people saw us carrying him for the story to have spread.'

As if to prove his words, the animal-skin curtain that hung across the doorway to the hut was pushed aside and Urien, a chief from the Silures, strode in, flanked by two of his warriors. Urien glared at the unconscious figure on the bed.

'I hear a Roman spy has been washed up!' he growled.

'We don't know for sure he is Roman,' said Drustan. 'And he's little more than a boy. I'd say about twelve or thirteen.'

Urien strode to the boy, bent over him and took a deep breath.

'He smells Roman!' he snarled.

'That's what I said,' the younger man put in.

Urien drew his sword. 'So, he dies!'

Drustan stepped quickly between Urien and the bed. 'Put your sword away!' he snapped, glowering menacingly at the Silures warrior. 'You are in my house.'

Urien hesitated, then reluctantly pushed his sword back into its scabbard. 'He is a Roman!' he argued.

'As I said, we don't know that for sure. But if he is, it's even more important that we keep him alive so that we can find out what the Romans are planning.'

'We know what they're planning!' stormed Urien. 'To invade this island and kill us all.'

'When? And with how large a force?' said Drustan. 'The more we know, the better we can prepare.'

Urien hesitated, then shook his head. 'We shall let the Council decide his fate,' he snapped.

With that, he swept out of the tent, and the others followed him.

Drustan looked to where Aithne was rubbing ointment into the unconscious boy's back.

'I will go and talk to the Council,' he told her, 'before Urien persuades them that the boy must die.'

Chapter 2
Castus

Slowly, Castus came round. He was lying face down on a bed of skins. He was in a small hut lit by torches and a fire. He was aware of hands rubbing ointments into his back. He began to turn but a girl's voice said, 'Lie still.'

Her hands moved away and then placed more of the warm ointment on his back and began to smooth it over his skin.

He sniffed, trying to identify the ointment. A plant of some sort, he was sure.

'Woundwort,' the girl said.

A bolt of fear shot through Castus. He had not spoken a word, and yet she had answered his unspoken question as if reading his thoughts. Was this the Druid magic he had heard spoken of? Yet he knew that the Druids were men. Was this one of the Wise Women of which the Gauls spoke? But surely the Wise Women were ancient.

He half-turned his head to look at the girl in the flickering light. This was no old woman. She looked to be about his own age, twelve.

He fought to keep the fear from rising up in him. This girl had read his mind. Was she reading his thoughts now? Did she know that he was on a secret mission, that the marks of the whip on his back were part of the plan to make the Britons believe he really was a runaway slave?

This was his chance to prove himself worthy to be a soldier. That was what the great commander himself, Suetonius Paulinus, chosen by the Emperor to be the Governor of Britannia, had told him on that fateful day when he had summoned Castus to his tent.

Castus had known nothing but the Roman army ever since he was born. His father, Antonius, had been a Roman centurion and his mother, Gwen, a British tribeswoman. Castus knew that it was unusual for Roman soldiers to marry British tribeswomen, but that is what Castus's father had done. Antonius had obviously loved her very much. Castus remembered how angry his father became if any of the other soldiers said anything against the Britons.

'They are human beings, just like us!' his father had shouted angrily at a fellow soldier once, when Castus had been just a child. The soldier had been making a joke about Britons being more stupid than sheep.

Things had changed for Castus when he was nine years old. His father had been killed in a battle with the Britons, and shortly afterwards his mother had fallen ill and died. Castus had been taken in by another centurion in the army, Comus, and his wife Minerva. Their attitudes towards the Britons were very different from those of Antonius.

'The Britons behave like wild animals,' Comus said.

'Worse,' said Minerva. 'And they say trees are sacred!' She looked at him and gave an unhappy sigh. 'Poor Castus,' she said. 'What a pity you look more like your mother than your father.'

From that moment, Castus had been determined to show that he had more of his Roman father in him than he did of his British mother. He echoed what Comus and Minerva said about the Britons. The Britons behaved like animals. Only Romans were civilized. And he was a Roman, like his father. And one day, like his father, he would join the Roman army as a soldier.

When he'd been ordered to the tent of the Governor, he'd felt confused. On one hand he'd been proud that the Governor himself had summoned him. But then nervousness had crept over him. Was it because he'd done something wrong?

Suetonius's manner had been quietly thoughtful. 'How old are you, boy?' he asked.

'I am twelve, sir.'

'Centurion Comus tells me you wish to join the army as soon as you are old enough.'

'Yes, sir!' answered Castus enthusiastically. 'It is my greatest ambition. I wish to serve Rome as my father did, and as my guardian Comus does!'

Suetonius nodded. 'I have had good reports about you

from Comus, and from those you work under.' Castus worked mostly in the kitchens, but also with the smiths in the armoury, making and repairing weapons. 'But being a soldier requires more than hard work. It needs courage when facing the enemy.'

'I have that courage, sir!' insisted Castus. 'I cannot wait until the day I see action!'

Suetonius studied him. 'That day may come sooner than you think. Are you prepared to face the enemy today?'

Castus's heart leaped with excitement. He couldn't believe it. The Governor was giving him the chance to go into battle against the Britons, even at his young age! He could avenge his father's death.

'Yes, sir!' said Castus, almost wanting to shout the answer out.

Suetonius nodded.

'You know we are preparing to attack the Britons gathered on the Isle of Mona across the water,' he said.

'Yes, sir.'

'Once we have crushed them, the rebellion will be ended, and Britannia will be ours completely.' He gave a half-smile as he added dismissively, 'That will leave the Caledonians in the north, of course, but we will deal with them once we have vanquished the rest.' He looked intently at Castus. 'That is why it is important that this mission does not fail. We have to eradicate these rebel Britons and their accursed Druid masters. The problem is, we do not have enough information about them, such as how many warriors they have, where their different camps are on the island and where their weak points are.'

He rose from his chair and stood towering over Castus.

'I could send a soldier as a spy, but he would soon be spotted as a Roman. I need someone who looks like a Briton. I am told you resemble your mother. Do you know which tribe she came from?'

'She was from the Dobunni,' replied Castus, uncomfortable at having to admit that he came from British stock.

'Very well,' said Suetonius. 'I have a mission for you. If you complete it successfully, it will go a long way to gaining you entry into the Roman army. You are to swim to Mona. Once there, you will tell them your name is Caradoc. It is a British name. Tell them that you are from the Dobunni tribe and have been kept as a slave by the Romans, but you have escaped to join the Silures rebellion. They will ask you about our strength here in the camp, and many other things. They will ask you when we plan to attack. You will tell them we do not attack for a week. That will lull them into a false feeling of security.

'After you have arrived on the island, a soldier from

the legion will also swim across, and will hide himself here.' Suetonius strode to a map of the island and pointed to a small cove. 'You will observe the British defences and report to him. He will swim back and, with that information, we will be able to prepare our invasion. Can you do this?'

'Yes, sir!' said Castus. He found he was trembling with excitement. Such a great responsibility! He felt proud that he had been chosen for this task, and by the Governor himself.

'You will need proof that you hate us Romans,' added Suetonius. 'You will be whipped, enough to convince the Britons that you have been punished and desire revenge. Have you been whipped before?'

'Yes, sir,' admitted Castus unhappily. 'When I was younger and had behaved badly. Centurion Comus said I needed to be whipped to learn discipline.' Quietly, Castus added: 'He said my own father had been too lax with me.'

Suetonius nodded.

'Centurion Comus is right. Discipline and bravery are the most important qualities in any army.' He patted Castus on the shoulder. 'Tonight, you will be whipped. Then you will rest to regain your strength, and at first light tomorrow you will swim across to Mona.' He paused, then added: 'It is up to you to make sure the Britons believe you are a runaway slave. If they do not, they will kill you. The marks of the whip will help, but it will be up to you to persuade them.

'Spend tomorrow observing them and their camp, and then at dusk tomorrow evening, meet the soldier who waits for you at the cove and tell him all you have found.'

'Am I to swim back with him, sir?' asked Castus.

'No,' said Suetonius. 'If you were to disappear, it would rouse their suspicions. We will attack shortly after we receive your report.'

And so Castus had been whipped, a torture he had endured for the sake of the mission. Then he had swum the cold waters of the Strait to the island. Or, almost swum the Strait. Cold and exhaustion had taken hold of him as he neared the island, and he'd passed out, waking here in this tent with the girl massaging ointment into his back.

Her gentle hands and soothing voice brought back memories of his mother. The way she had laughed. Her touch. The looks of affection between his father and his mother, that he'd almost forgotten.

The sound of skins rustling as someone came in made the girl stop and look towards the entrance of the hut. Into Castus's line of vision came a man, a warrior.

'How is the prisoner, Aithne?' asked the man.

'He will recover,' said the girl. 'He is strong.'

'Then let him use his strength to rise,' said the man. 'The Council wish to see him.'

Chapter 3
The Council

Castus followed the man through the village. Warrior Britons accompanied them, keeping him under close guard. Castus stumbled along, struggling as if in pain. In truth, he was already feeling much stronger, but it would not do to let these Britons know that. Better that they considered him weak and frail and no danger to anyone. It was strange how the pain of his whipped back seemed to have eased. Was it the woundwort that the girl had rubbed into it?

As Castus limped along under guard, children appeared at the doors of the huts to watch him pass. They had obviously heard of his arrival on the island, this 'dead body' from the sea that now walked.

At the far end of the village they arrived at a small group of huts and halted before the largest.

'Enter.' The warrior on guard motioned Castus in.

The hut was large, but most of the torchlight was centred on a bare patch of earth by the central post, where seven men sat in a semicircle. Each man stared at Castus as he was pushed forward by the warriors into the light.

The garments of five of the men were adorned with golden torcs and bronze amulets. From their weapons Castus guessed they were tribal chiefs. Two of the seven, however, were dressed in coarse robes with no adornment. The elder of these two had long grey hair with a beard to match; his gaze seemed to see into Castus's very soul, and Castus felt a chill. The girl had read his thoughts. Was this Druid now reading his soul?

The man with the grey hair was the first to speak. 'Who are you?' he asked.

Castus cleared his throat, then he said: 'My name is Caradoc.'

'He claims a British name,' commented one of the chiefs.

'Where are you from?' asked the other robed figure, the younger of the two Druids.

'I was a slave in the Roman camp across the water,' said Castus.

'Why did you come here?'

'Because I want to be free.'

'Who is your father?' This question came from one of the chiefs, a huge man with a scar that seemed to split his face in half from forehead to chin.

'I did not know him,' answered Castus. 'He died before I was born. All I know is that he was of the Dobunni tribe and he died fighting the Romans.'

'And your mother?'

'She, too, was of the Dobunni. She was taken into slavery by the Romans when I was small. She is also dead.'

The chief with the scar nodded. 'So, a Briton.'

'I say he smells Roman,' growled another chief.

'Of course he does, Urien,' retorted another chieftain with some annoyance. 'All Roman slaves do. It does not make them Roman.'

'He could be a spy,' growled Urien. 'Or does Drustan not consider that a possibility?'

The chief he'd addressed, Drustan, bridled at this attack on him. 'Turn him round and strip the clothes off his back,' he ordered. The warriors who had brought Castus to the Council hut stepped forward.

The skin cloak was unwrapped from Castus's body and his wounds were revealed to the assembly, the whip-marks criss-crossing his back, the blood mixed with the ointment.

'Look at his body! Do they look like the marks the Romans would make on one of their own?' demanded Drustan.

'They would if they wanted him to pass among us,' retorted Urien hotly.

'I believe that Urien is obsessed by spies,' said Drustan.

'Someone has to be,' Urien snapped back angrily. 'The Romans are just across the water, perhaps even now preparing to attack.'

The elder Druid looked at Castus.

'Are they?' he asked. 'Are the Romans preparing to attack us?'

Castus shook his head.

'No,' he said. 'We always know when they are preparing to attack. All troops are rested and well fed two days before a battle so that they will fight in good heart. There has been no such resting.'

The elder Druid looked at a chief who had so far sat in silence.

'What does Bretowen say to that?' he asked.

Bretowen nodded.

'He speaks the truth,' he said. 'These are Roman ways.'

'A Roman would know that also,' growled Urien, refusing to relinquish his argument.

Castus knew that although slaves should be silent, to remain so now was to risk his life. He must answer Urien.

'I am no Roman,' he said defiantly. 'If you kill me for my insolence in speaking when I should not, so be it. But the Romans killed my mother and my father. The Romans have kept me as a slave all my life. I loathe and despise the Romans.'

* * *

He's lying, realized Aithne.

She had been standing at the back of the hut near the entrance, watching and listening as the chiefs questioned the boy. There had been something false about the way he'd answered, as if he had been repeating things he'd been taught and had committed to memory, rather than things he'd experienced himself. But this last long speech of his had rung particularly false. The words had been fine, but the way he'd spoken them had sounded hollow.

She had to let her father know, but later, when he was away from the Council. She knew that if she aired her thoughts now, Urien would insist the boy was killed.

And I could be wrong, she told herself. *It could be that he's just scared, and that's affecting the way he speaks.*

She slipped out and headed back to her own hut. As she neared it, she saw a bird perched on the roof of the hut, and tied to one leg was a black feather.

It was a message. A cry for help.

Chapter 4
Flight

Drustan barged into the tent, a look of anger on his face.

'Urien questions my judgement!' he stormed. 'He seems to think he's the only chief with experience of battle on this island!'

He stopped as he saw that Aithne was sitting holding a black feather in her hand, a concerned expression on her face.

Aithne held the feather towards him.

'A bird brought it,' she said. 'It's from home.'

Drustan took the feather from her and studied it. A pale feather would mean the Iceni, their home tribe, were desperate for Drustan's warrior skills. A black feather meant they urgently needed Aithne's skills as a Wise Woman.

'I have to go,' she said. 'Someone must be ill.'

Herbs and potions had always been Aithne's special skill, from when she had been a small child. She had learned about them from her grandmother, her mother's mother, who was skilled in all medicines.

But her grandmother hadn't been able to save the life of Aithne's mother, who'd died giving birth to Aithne.

'You must learn everything there is, to stop that happening to anyone else,' her grandmother had told her. 'It is your duty to save people. You must be a healer.'

And so Aithne had studied plants of all sorts, those that healed and those that could harm: yarrow, that could stop bleeding and heal wounds; lemon verbena for reducing fever; chervil to treat rheumatism and gout; horseradish to treat infection. So many plants with such a range of healing powers.

Back home, Queen Boudicca had valued Aithne. Aithne had come to the aid of the Queen's daughters with herbal remedies and potions when they had fallen dangerously ill, and she had been able to save them when Seers and other Wise Women had failed.

An urgent message like this could only mean one thing. Someone was very sick.

But Drustan shook his head.

'You cannot go,' said Drustan. 'Away from this island there are many dangers. Not just from the Romans but from thieves.'

'Are we any safer here?' asked Aithne.

'No,' admitted Drustan. 'But here I can protect you.'

'You will not be able to protect me when the Romans come,' said Aithne. She stood up. 'I will leave now. I will use our coracle to get to the mainland. The sooner I start, the quicker I will get home.'

Drustan paced in the confines of the hut, a scowl on his face.

'I will be safe,' said Aithne. 'Safer than here. The Romans will attack, and soon. We are outnumbered. We will all die. At least if I go home, I can help our people.'

'I have never run from an enemy yet!' Drustan growled. 'But I will not let my daughter travel these dangerous roads unprotected.' He nodded to himself. 'And perhaps we can carry on the fight against the Romans there, on our own home ground. Perhaps the Iceni need us both.'

* * *

They carried very little to avoid rousing suspicion as they made their way to the shore, just their weapons and a goatskin of fresh water. They dragged their coracle from the grassy bank and across the shingle to the water's edge. Some small boys watched them, curious.

'Where are you going?' called one boy.

'Fishing,' said Drustan.

They pushed the coracle on to the water, then each took a paddle and set off, heading for the mainland, but taking an upstream course to avoid the Roman camp. As they paddled, Aithne looked back, and she saw a mass of barges on the shore just below the Roman camp.

'Look!' she called.

Her father turned and saw the barges, and the sun glinting on the armour and weapons of thousands of Roman soldiers who were assembling by them.

'The invasion!' he said. 'They are preparing! The boy was wrong!'

Or he lied, thought Aithne.

Chapter 5
The Journey Home

They paddled the coracle a good way along the Strait before heading for the mainland. Once ashore, at Drustan's suggestion, they decided to avoid the main Roman road that led south and east, and instead keep to quieter tracks.

'It will take longer, but we won't run the risk of coming up against a body of Romans on the march,' he said.

* * *

Their journey was a long one. Sometimes they walked, sometimes they begged rides on farm carts and wagons taking goods from town to town. At night they slept in barns, or in haystacks if no cover was available. As they journeyed, they kept their ears open for any information about what could be happening in the east, eager to find out what danger had prompted the sending of the black feather from Iceni territory.

'There's been some sort of uprising in the east,' one carter told them. But he didn't know who it was who'd risen up, and whether it was against the Romans, or an inter-tribal struggle. Here, in the north-west, most of the talk was about the Roman invasion of Mona.

'They say the Romans killed everyone on the island,' one wagon-driver told them. 'And they cut down the oak groves and burned them, as if they wanted to burn out all traces of the Druids so there'd be no more uprisings.'

Aithne and Drustan looked at one another, their faces ashen as they took in the full horror that had befallen Mona. Their friends, the children they'd watched playing, a whole community – all gone.

The carter shook his head. 'We're living in cruel times. And they'll get worse, you mark my words.'

As they moved further eastward, the gossip and talk changed. People spoke less about what had happened on Mona and more about events in the south-east.

'Riots and mayhem,' said one woman at an inn where they stopped. 'They say there's an army on the march against the Romans.'

'An army?' asked Drustan. 'Whose army?'

The woman shook her head. 'Not sure. Whoever it is, people say they've got the Romans on the run.'

They'd been on the road for a while, and were nearing the borders of the eastern kingdoms, before they learned the truth of the situation.

A carter called Dirk, a cheerful man taking a supply of cloth south to Londinium, picked them up. 'I can take you as far as the Great Road,' he told them.

'That will be fine,' said Drustan. 'We thank you.'

He and Aithne joined Dirk on the seat at the front of the cart, and the carter flicked the reins, urging his two horses onward.

'Iceni, eh?' said Dirk.

Drustan nodded.

'Thought so,' said Dirk with a smug smile. 'It was the handle of your sword that told me. The pattern. When you travel the roads as much as I do you meet all sorts, see all the different designs of the leather and sword hilts. So, I'm guessing you're on your way to join Queen Boudicca in the uprising. Lots are, and not just Iceni. Trinovantes. Catuvellauni. Everyone's flocking to her.'

'What uprising?' asked Drustan.

Dirk looked at him in surprise. 'You're Iceni and you don't know what's happening with your own people?'

'We've been away,' said Aithne quickly. 'In another part of the country. For a long while.'

'How long you been away?' asked Dirk.

'It's been three years,' replied Aithne.

'Then you'll definitely find that everything's changed,' said Dirk. 'Prasutagus was king then, right? Well, he's dead, and he left his kingdom to be split equally between Rome and his daughters.'

Drustan's expression soured. Aithne assumed he was remembering how Prasutagus had given over control of the Iceni territory to the Romans in exchange for remaining king. A handful of Iceni warrior chiefs had left their homeland rather than submit to Roman rule. Drustan had been one of them. 'The trouble started when the Roman Provincial Procurator, Catus Decianus, declared he was going to ignore the will, even though it had been agreed,' Dirk continued. 'Under Roman law a woman can't inherit property.'

'Why can't she?' asked Aithne.

'Who knows why the Romans think the way they do,' Drustan shrugged. 'Britons see women as being just as important as men. More so, in some cases, as with Wise Women like yourself. But for the Romans, women don't have any rights.'

'That makes no sense,' said Aithne with a sigh.

'Anyway, the new leader, Catus, said he was taking the whole Iceni territory for Rome,' Dirk told them. 'What that meant, of course, was he was taking it for himself. Looting it.'

'I warned Prasutagus he couldn't trust the Romans,' Drustan muttered to Aithne.

Dirk continued: 'Catus moved in with a small force of soldiers. His men looted the houses of Iceni nobles, and imprisoned the Queen and her two daughters.' He gave a shake of his head. 'He brought about his own downfall. Boudicca escaped, vowing vengeance, and urged the Iceni and other neighbouring tribes to rise up against Roman oppression. The Romans weren't prepared for it. Next thing, Boudicca had gathered a small army, and before the Romans knew what was happening, she attacked Camulodonum.'

'The capital!' said Drustan, stunned.

'Yes. And Boudicca's army won,' said Dirk. 'The Romans fled. They say that Catus got so scared of what Boudicca would do to him if she caught him, he set sail for Gaul.'

'So she drove the Romans out of Iceni territory,' said Drustan, awed. He looked at Aithne and grinned. 'I always knew she was a warrior, but I never thought she'd go that far.'

'She's gone farther than that,' said Dirk. 'After she forced the Romans out of Iceni lands, she marched on Londinium. And because word had spread that she'd driven the Romans out of Camulodonum, everyone who wanted the Romans out of Britannia flocked to join her. Thousands of them. By the time her army reached Londinium they reckon it was over two hundred thousand strong.'

'Two hundred thousand!' echoed Drustan.

Dirk nodded. 'And growing all the time. People say she's got about a quarter of a million with her now. It's not just warriors. There are whole families with her. Children. Women. Old people. It's more a city on the move than a proper army. Wagons and everything.'

'What happened when they reached Londinium?' asked Aithne.

'They destroyed it,' answered Dirk. 'Killed everyone. Torched the place. Same happened when they got to Verulamium.'

'But what about the Roman army?' asked Aithne. 'Did Boudicca defeat them at Londinium and Verulamium as well?'

'No, the Roman troops fled both places before her army got there,' said Dirk. 'Abandoned both Londinium and Verulamium. The Roman army is on the run!'

* * *

Shortly afterwards, they arrived at the Great Road.

'This is as far as I take you,' Dirk said. 'I'm heading south from here, and if you want to catch up with Queen Boudicca and her army, you need to head northwards.'

'How far north are they?' asked Drustan, getting down from the wagon.

'Just follow the Roman road,' said Dirk. 'Let's face it, an army of a quarter of a million people ain't going to be hard to find.' He looked at the road stretching in both directions, wide and straight, and gave an approving smile. 'Mind, you can say what you like about the Romans, but they do make a beautiful road!'

Chapter 6
The Warriors Gather

Aithne and Drustan moved from bush to bush, selecting fruits, nuts and berries which they laid out on her cloak. Aithne knew which ones were safe to eat.

'This will keep us going for a while,' said Aithne. 'But later we must hunt.'

As they ate, Drustan continued to reflect on what he'd heard about Boudicca's uprising.

'She has done wonders,' he marvelled. 'To drive the Roman army out of Camulodonum, then force them to flee Londinium and Verulamium! Something we were never able to do when we were fighting the Romans before!' He munched on an apple. 'If Boudicca had led us instead of Prasutagus, I'd never have left.'

'It seems she is driving more than the Romans out,' said Aithne guardedly. 'If what Dirk said is right, she's been killing civilians. Including British civilians. Our own people.'

'I can't believe that,' he said. 'Those are stories spread by our enemies to discredit her and our people.' He shook his head and said in awe, 'An army a quarter of a million strong! If we'd had them with us on Mona, we could have crushed the Romans. Driven them out of Britannia.' He looked sad. 'All those brave warriors on Mona, lost.'

Then he scowled, angry. 'I should have stayed! I could have led them!'

'The Romans would still have won,' said Aithne. 'One more warrior would have made no difference. Not even a great warrior like you could have stopped what was going to happen on Mona. One thousand Britons, including women and children, against five thousand Roman soldiers.'

'If only they could have held the Romans off until Boudicca and her army arrived!' said Drustan, agonized.

'*If*,' said Aithne, shaking her head. 'If a cow had wings it could fly. There was no time for Boudicca to arrive on Mona before the Romans invaded. Even now, she's still only making her way north.'

Drustan nodded, and heaved a sorrowful sigh. 'You're right, of course.'

'The important thing is that we're alive, and we can join with her in taking the fight to the Romans,' Aithne told him.

'And this time, we'll win!' said Drustan firmly. 'And we'll avenge all those who died on Mona!'

'Father!' interrupted Aithne urgently as four dirt-stained men appeared from the trees, one carrying a short sword, two others holding spears, and the fourth carrying a club.

But Drustan's warrior instincts had warned him already, for as soon as he heard the rustle of branches, he turned to face them, drawing his sword.

The four men stopped, exchanged looks then advanced again, warily and with looks of grim determination on their faces, although Aithne noticed that they looked frail, all of them almost on the point of collapse.

'All we want is food!' shouted one.

Drustan laughed. 'There is food all around you!' he retorted. 'Fruits on the trees. Roots in the ground.'

'We do not know which ones are good and which will poison us,' said another.

'They are not warriors, Father,' Aithne muttered. 'They are townsfolk.'

Warriors would have spread out, coming at their enemy from different directions. These men had grouped together for safety, because they were frightened and inexperienced away from the safety of the town.

Drustan nodded. 'Put down your weapons!' he commanded. 'If you come any nearer I will be forced to kill you.'

'He is a warrior,' Aithne heard one of the men murmur to his companions.

'He is more than that,' said Aithne loudly. 'He is Drustan, warrior chief of the Iceni, with more than a hundred victories in battle. Inexperienced men such as yourselves, even with four of you, will be no match for the two of us.'

'Two?' queried one of the men, puzzled.

Aithne patted her robe. 'I, too, am armed, and have learned much about fighting from my father.'

The men stopped, now very uncertain.

'Where are you from and why do you try to rob peaceful travellers?' asked Aithne.

One of the men gave a mocking laugh. 'Peaceful travellers?' he said sarcastically. 'We are from Verulamium. It was the Iceni who attacked us and killed our people and burned our houses!'

'You are Romans,' said Drustan.

The man shook his head. 'We are Britons, but because we live in a Roman town alongside Romans, your Queen Boudicca and her Iceni army came and destroyed us.'

'This cannot be!' said Drustan, shaking his head. 'Boudicca fights only the Romans.'

'She counts anyone who works for them as Roman!' shouted the man. 'I was a baker. I baked bread. Romans bought it.'

'And I built houses,' said another. He began to cry. 'And for that, the Iceni killed my family.'

Aithne moved towards the men, and as they saw this they backed away, frightened.

'Do not kill us!' said one. He gestured towards the trees. 'We have children who depend on us. We need food for them.'

Aithne looked, and saw the small figures of children looking out nervously from behind the trees.

'I was not going to harm you,' she said. 'I was coming to give you food.'

Nervously, the men hesitated, then they came forward and took the fruits and nuts she held out.

'Keep some of them so you will know what to pick in the future,' she said. 'And my advice is to go now, and keep to the forests. These are dangerous times and not everyone you meet will be as generous towards you.'

'Go west,' said Drustan suddenly. 'There is no rebellion against the Romans there ... yet.'

'Thank you,' said the man with the sword.

Holding the food that Aithne had given them, they headed back towards the trees, and the children. Aithne and Drustan watched them go.

'I still don't believe it,' said Drustan grimly. 'They were attacked by rebels out of control, not by Boudicca!'

Aithne didn't reply. It had been a long time since her father had seen the Queen. People could change.

* * *

They headed north. They'd walked three miles before a wagon pulled up beside them. Two men sat on the driver's seat – one older, bearded and muscular, the other younger, clean-shaven and thin. There were two women and four children in the back of the wagon.

The women and children were dressed in rough clothes, the men's bodies painted with patterns in blue woad. Aithne saw the swords, shields and spears piled in the back of the wagon, along with their belongings.

'I'm guessing you're on your way to join Boudicca,' said the older of the men.

'We are,' nodded Drustan.

'Then you are welcome to travel with us,' said the man. 'We, too, go to join the army that will drive the Romans out. My name is Axel. This is my brother, Torix.' He gestured at the people in the cart. 'Our wives, Brona and Oona, and our children.'

Drustan introduced himself and Aithne.

'A Wise Woman,' observed Axel, spotting the silver mooncrest brooch on Aithne's dress as Drustan and Aithne climbed aboard. 'And Iceni?'

'We are,' confirmed Drustan.

'Yet you are not already with Boudicca?' questioned Axel, a tone of suspicion in his voice.

'We have been away battling the Romans elsewhere,' explained Drustan. 'We've only just received a message summoning us.'

Axel nodded. 'Then it is your fortune we came along.'

'And yours, if we are attacked,' said Drustan, patting his sword.

'If what we hear is true, we won't be coming up against any Romans before we meet with Boudicca's army,' said Axel. 'The Romans are running before them like scared dogs.' He grinned. 'Their days are numbered!'

Chapter 7
Boudicca's Army

Axel gestured for his younger brother, Torix, to join the women and children in the back of the cart, so that Drustan could sit next to him on the driver's seat. Axel was obviously eager to hear more about the great Queen Boudicca from this Iceni warrior. Aithne joined the others in the back of the cart and tried to engage them in conversation, but none of them, including Torix, seemed to want to talk. Looking at the sullen expressions on their faces, Aithne got the impression that none of them wanted to be there, but had been pressured to come along.

Axel, however, was keen to talk.

'You know Boudicca?' he asked.

'I do,' replied Drustan. 'I was one of King Prasutagus's warrior chiefs who fought against the Romans, before Prasutagus decided to surrender and throw in his lot with them.'

'A traitor!' hissed Axel.

'He did what he thought was best for his people,' said Drustan sourly. 'He got what he believed were good terms: independence, of a sort.'

'But still under Roman rule?' grunted Axel.

'Unfortunately,' nodded Drustan.

'And you left?' asked Axel.

'I did,' said Drustan. 'My daughter and I left to join those tribes who were still resisting the Romans.'

'We are Cantiaci, and our King was the first to surrender when the Romans came,' said Axel bitterly. Then he brightened. 'But now the time has come for us to join the Iceni and put those years of shame behind us.'

* * *

The first signs that they had found Boudicca's army were the stationary carts and wagons along the road. Some of the carts had been pulled into wooded areas to give shelter beneath the trees. Horses and oxen, unharnessed, grazed alongside. Dusk was falling and the flames from campfires flickered in the fading light.

Axel drove on past, but at the crest of the next hill he hauled on the reins. 'I've never seen anything like this!' he said, awed.

Aithne looked over his shoulder, and shook her head in wonder at the sight before them: thousands of carts and wagons, and tens of thousands of people sitting on them or by them, as far as the eye could see.

When Dirk the carter had said that Boudicca's army numbered a quarter of a million, Aithne had been sceptical. Warriors always exaggerated their strengths to try and unsettle the enemy. But this was no exaggeration. Aithne had never seen this many people in one place in all her life, not when her father had taken her to Camulodonum or Londinium when she was younger, nor when there had been a gathering of tribes for a celebration. This was truly immense. A quarter of a million people!

'No wonder the Romans are running,' chuckled Axel. 'Every free Briton in the whole country must be here!' He turned to Drustan. 'We'll find a place to park our wagon. It's too congested further ahead.'

Drustan nodded. 'We thank you for bringing us this far,' he said. 'We'll walk on and find our people.'

'Queen Boudicca herself?' asked Axel.

'At least her warrior chiefs,' said Drustan.

He clambered down from the cart, and Aithne joined him.

'Perhaps we'll meet again, after we've driven the Romans out,' said Axel.

'Perhaps we will,' nodded Drustan. 'I wish you all well.'

As he and Aithne set off along the road, heading for the bulk of the huge army a mile or so further on, Aithne said: 'Axel is keen, but the others with him are unhappy.'

'I know,' said Drustan. 'I saw their faces too. They are not warriors. They just want a life with no battles. And

Axel, for all his body paint and talk, is no warrior either. I fear for them once the fighting starts.'

They walked on, past whole family groups gathered around campfires, eating and making merry.

'They are celebrating already,' said Aithne thoughtfully.

'Understandably,' said Drustan. 'No Roman army can withstand this many people, no matter how much armour they hide behind. We will crush the Romans by sheer weight of numbers.'

The further they walked, the thicker the masses of people became, and familiar banners and signs began to appear.

'Our people!' smiled Drustan.

The Iceni were right at the front, as was to be expected. This was Boudicca's rebellion, led by her.

'Drustan! Is that you?'

The shout made them stop. Two Iceni warrior chiefs had appeared from a circle of wagons and were hurrying towards them. Both wore cloaks of hides pinned with gold fastenings that glinted in the light of the campfires, and each had a longsword dangling from his belt.

'Garth! Trey!' Drustan called back delightedly.

The taller of the two, Garth, moved with a pronounced limp, and Drustan remembered the battle against the Romans in which he'd been maimed. The other, Trey, was a short wiry man, but even more adorned with gold decorations than Garth.

The three warriors greeted one another warmly.

'And Aithne, you've grown since I last saw you!' Garth smiled at Aithne. Then he frowned. 'But you were on Mona!'

'We were,' nodded Drustan. 'Until Aithne received a feather.'

'The Queen summoned you?'

'I don't know if it was the Queen who sent it,' said Aithne. 'All I knew was, it was a message calling for my help.'

'It was the Queen,' said Trey firmly. 'She sent out messages summoning all her Wise Women. She is making a Council of them, along with Seers, to give her the power to finally push the Romans out of this country.'

'I wouldn't have thought she'd have needed such a Council,' commented Drustan, looking at the assembled throng, the campfires, the wagons, stretching for miles back along the Roman road. 'Not with an army as big as this.'

'We have yet to meet the main body of the Roman army,' said Garth. 'Suetonius Paulinus's troops.'

'Come, Aithne,' said Trey. 'Leave these two to talk battle tactics. I'll take you to Boudicca's wagon. She will be eager to see you.'

'Give the Queen my greetings and tell her I have come here to serve her,' said Drustan.

Trey nodded, and he and Aithne headed off through the mass of tents, carts, wagons and people.

* * *

Once they had gone, Drustan turned to Garth and murmured: 'Something worries you, old friend.'

45

'Worries me?' repeated Garth. He gave a small smile. 'Why should I be worried? My warrior friend, Drustan, has returned to join me. We have the Romans on the run.'

Drustan shook his head.

'You cannot fool me, Garth. I know you too well. Despite all these victories – the biggest victories we Britons have ever known against the Roman invaders – you seem ... unsettled. What is wrong?'

Garth hesitated, then he leaned in toward Drustan and whispered: 'Things are not as they appear.'

Chapter 8
Warriors Reunited

Garth looked about them to make sure they couldn't be overheard. He kept his voice low. 'When you and I went into battle, we fought as warriors against warriors. This army of Boudicca's is a mob: men who are not soldiers, women, children, all raised to levels of passion by her anger against the Romans. A rabble.'

'I saw them as we walked along the road,' nodded Drustan. 'And I agree, it does look like a mob, rather than an army. But it is a large mob.'

'Too large for a handful of retired old soldiers to handle,' said Garth. 'And that's who we faced at Camulodonum. Old soldiers who were past their prime and who'd settled down in the city.'

'Why only them?' asked Drustan, puzzled. 'Where were the regular soldiers of the garrison?'

'Gone to join Suetonius Paulinus for his attack on Mona,' said Garth. 'He took all the fittest serving soldiers.'

'A whole army,' nodded Drustan bitterly.

'Were you in the battle?' asked Garth.

Drustan shook his head.

'We left before they attacked, when Aithne received the feather asking for help. But as we left, we saw the Romans massing ready to invade.'

'We received word,' said Garth. 'Mona is lost. There were no survivors. Suetonius even had the sacred oak woods on the island cut down and burned, because he feared Druids from Ireland might gather there.'

Suddenly they heard footsteps. Garth signalled to Drustan to keep silent, his hand poised over his sword. He relaxed when he saw it was Trey returning.

'I have delivered Aithne to the Queen,' said Trey. 'Boudicca expressed her pleasure at Aithne's return. She said she needs her Wise Women for guidance.'

'Guidance!' echoed Garth, a note of derision in his voice. 'We know who we will face – Suetonius and his best soldiers. If she needs guidance it should be from us, her warriors.'

Trey frowned and gave Garth a warning look, but Garth said: 'Drustan is one of us, Trey. I have been telling him the truth of the so-called glorious victory at Camulodonum.'

'Against old soldiers past their prime,' nodded Drustan.

'That's not the worst,' muttered Trey.

He gestured for them to sit, glancing around to check there was still no one in earshot. 'When the Romans ran away, Boudicca ordered the destruction of many ordinary houses and villages,' said Trey.

'But there would have been Britons living in those villages, our own people!' said Drustan, shocked.

He remembered the ragged men they'd come upon in the woods. He had dismissed their stories.

'We counselled against it,' said Trey. 'But the Queen insisted that any Briton who lived alongside the Romans, or worked with them, was a traitor.'

'But the Queen herself shared her rule with the Romans when her husband was alive,' said Drustan.

'That was always against her wishes,' Garth reminded him. 'She disagreed with his policy, believing he should have resisted the Romans more; but he was king. His word was law.'

'But why has she become so ... vengeful?' asked Drustan. 'I agree she always wanted to resist the Roman occupation, but there was no sign of this ... this crazed bloodthirstiness before. She was a warrior, like us. And fair.'

'It was the Roman Provincial Procurator's doing,' said Garth. 'Catus Decianus. After King Prasutagus died, Catus became greedy. He didn't want to share the kingdom of the Iceni with Prasutagus's daughters; he wanted it all. The whole territory, so he could loot it for his personal gain.'

'He put Boudicca and her two daughters in prison,' added Trey. He shook his head. 'I don't know what happened to them while they were in there, but whatever it was, it must have been something very bad. It changed her. Before, Boudicca was a proud but fair warrior queen. After she got out, she was obsessed with vengeance, and has been ever since. So we're left attacking old Romans and our own people.'

'You could refuse,' said Drustan. 'You are warriors. You could refuse to attack our own people.'

'And be called traitors by her and the mob she rules?' said Trey. 'Driven out, or perhaps killed.' He shook his head. 'I refuse to give up on our people, Drustan. The Iceni are a noble tribe. I want to be around when they are restored to greatness, but by honest means.'

They heard footsteps approach, light ones, and they looked up to see one of Boudicca's Wise Women approaching.

'Chief Drustan,' she said. She gave him a small smile, but Drustan noticed it wasn't echoed in her eyes, which remained wary and suspicious. 'The Queen asks that you join her. Your daughter is already with her.'

Drustan stood up and bowed.

'It will be my pleasure,' he said.

Chapter 9
Boudicca

It had been three years since Aithne had last seen Boudicca. Then, the Queen had mainly been involved, along with King Prasutagus, in sorting out disputes between individual members of the Iceni tribe: a row about who owned a sheep or a cow, or a claim by one tribal member that their reputation had been sullied by another. The Romans, although officially the conquering power, were not much in evidence, content to leave the day-to-day running of thc kingdom to the King and Queen and their advisers. Providing taxes and levies were paid, usually in the form of livestock and grain, the Romans left the Iceni to their own devices.

That had not been enough for her father, who loathed the fact that they had to pay taxes to the invaders – part of their hard-earned labour was being stolen, as far as Drustan was concerned. Furthermore, whatever decisions the Iceni King made about his people's lives, the Roman Governor always had the final say. The Britons did not have the freedom to decide their own fates. That was why her father had left to continue his fight against the Romans on his own, taking Aithne with him. They bade farewell to Prasutagus and Boudicca, and departed with their royal blessing – although even that had been given secretly for fear of angering the Romans.

But that was then. Now, the stance that Boudicca adopted as Aithne entered her wagon – tense, her features hard, her eyes glittering with a fierce light – showed that those days of royal submission to the Romans were gone.

'Aithne!'

Boudicca's face softened, but only momentarily. Although her mouth smiled in warm welcome, her eyes showed the glitter of vengeance.

'I received your message, my Queen,' said Aithne, and bowed.

'You do not need to bow, Aithne,' murmured Boudicca. 'You are one of my most favoured Wise Women. And grown older.'

'We came as soon as we could,' said Aithne.

'We?'

'My father, Drustan, is with me.'

'Ah, Drustan!' Boudicca's smile broadened. 'The bravest warrior. The one who dared to oppose the Romans when others – including my late husband – said we must bow down to them. Well, no more! You have seen my army?'

'Yes, my Queen,' said Aithne. 'A powerful force, indeed.'

'And growing larger every day! As I forecast it would. We saw the signs, my Wise Women and my Seers.' She half-turned. 'You remember Nova?'

Aithne looked at the slight figure of the Wise Woman who moved forward from the shadows at the back of the wagon. *Yes,* she thought bitterly, *I remember Nova only too well.* Nova looked about eighteen now. She had been a nasty piece of work, bullying Aithne and the other girls, but doing it in a clever way, pretending to be their caring friend when adults were around, but vicious when they were absent: name-calling, skin-pinching, hair-pulling, terrorizing. She'd wormed her way into the Queen's inner circle, claiming mystical powers as a Wise Woman, especially prophecy; and when some of those prophecies came true – mainly because Nova manipulated things to make sure they happened – she'd been given more power to bully. She'd cemented her place by spreading gossip and telling lies about the others in the Queen's inner circle; but she had never managed to discredit Aithne in the Queen's eyes.

Because I saved Boudicca's daughters a few years ago, thought Aithne. *A parent doesn't forget such a thing.*

Now Aithne became aware of two other women at the back of the wagon, both wearing the mooncrest brooch that identified them as Wise Women. Bex and Riana, whom she remembered as Nova's henchwomen.

So these three, Nova, Bex and Riana, were now Boudicca's inner circle, her advisers.

'Riana, go and find Aithne's father Drustan, and bring him here to me,' commanded Boudicca.

'Yes, my Queen.'

'You'll find him with Garth and Trey,' said Aithne.

As Riana left, Nova turned to Aithne and said quizzically: 'We understood that everyone on Mona had been killed by the Romans.'

'We left before they attacked,' said Aithne.

'You ran away?' said Nova, putting on a tone of surprise. 'Unusual for a warrior such as Drustan.'

Aithne did her best to remain calm and not let Nova goad her.

'We left as soon as we received the Queen's message,' she said. 'A summons from the Queen overrides everything else, as I'm sure you'll agree.'

'My Aithne!' smiled Boudicca. 'Loyal as ever! You must join me here on my wagon with the rest of my inner council. I will need your thoughts and guidance more than ever, as we approach the final battle with the Romans.' Boudicca's eyes gleamed as she leaned forward intently. 'A battle which we shall win, with your help!'

The curtain parted and Riana returned. Behind her came Drustan.

'You sent for me, my Queen,' he said, and bowed.

'Now we are complete!' said Boudicca. 'You were always the best of our Iceni warriors, Drustan. Garth and Trey and the others have their uses, but they do not have your passionate hatred of the Romans. The passion that took you to Mona to continue the fight, when it seemed that we Iceni had capitulated to them in our homeland.' Suddenly she shouted out: 'But we never did! My husband may have! But not I!' Just as quickly her tone softened as she said: 'It went hard on Mona, we are told.'

Drustan's face was solemn. 'It did, my Queen. But, because Aithne had received your feather message summoning us, we left before the Romans attacked.'

'Yes, so Aithne has told us,' said Boudicca. 'You will be avenged, Drustan. *We* will be avenged!' But then she swayed. She reached out and took hold of one of the wagon's wooden struts. 'I will rest now,' she said, looking tired. 'You will come to my wagon again in the morning, Aithne.'

'Yes, my Queen,' bowed Aithne.

Aithne and Drustan left the wagon. As they climbed down the wooden steps on to the grass, they were aware that Nova had followed them.

'I wish to talk privately with Aithne,' said Nova to Drustan, her tone curt.

Drustan nodded. 'I will see you at Garth and Trey's camp,' he said to Aithne.

He nodded farewell to Nova, and disappeared among the clusters of tents and makeshift shelters. As soon as he had gone, Nova turned on Aithne, her face twisted in anger.

'You should have died on Mona!' she spat.

'But I did not,' replied Aithne calmly, aware that responding with the same kind of hatred would only make Nova even angrier.

'You are not welcome here, Aithne!' snarled Nova.

'Our Queen seems to welcome me,' said Aithne.

'Our Queen!' mimicked Nova with a sneer. Then anger filled her face again. 'You were always her favourite. Well, no more! *I* am her favoured Wise Woman now. *I* sit at her right hand. She listens to *my* counsel.'

'I am not here to take your position, Nova,' said Aithne. 'I came because the Queen summoned me. I have no ambition to be part of the royal court.'

Nova shook her head.

'I do not trust you, Aithne. No one is as "nice" as you pretend to be. I hear your words, but I know in your heart *you* desire to be the Queen's favourite, to sit beside her and bask in her glory. Well, you won't! That place is mine! And if you try to take it from me, I will finish you!'

With that, Nova turned on her heel and hurried back to Boudicca's wagon. Aithne watched her go.

Nova is a dangerous person. I have to be careful, Aithne told herself.

She was just about to head towards Garth and Trey's camp, when she saw a familiar shape standing beside a campfire. Her heart gave a sudden jolt. Even seeing him from the back, she knew it was him.

The boy from Mona. Caradoc. The liar.

Chapter 10
Caradoc

Castus recognized her voice at once, even though she'd only said a few words to him when she was rubbing ointment into his back. Instantly a bolt of fear shot through him. Aithne, the girl from Mona! He would have to be careful what he said in her presence. Perhaps he could pretend he hadn't heard or seen her and vanish into the crowd. Perhaps she'd think she'd been mistaken. But no, she was a Wise Woman. She had a Power. He had to get away. Hide!

But even as he began to move, he felt her hand on his arm.

'Caradoc.'

Slowly, terrified, he turned to face her, forcing a look of surprise on to his face.

'You escaped, too!' he burst out.

She looked at him, her face sad, and shook her head.

'You lie again, as you did on Mona,' she said.

'No!' he protested.

'Yes,' she said. 'I know what you are. A spy.'

At these words, he almost collapsed.

'No, please!' he begged. 'I was, but I am no longer.'

'Then why are you here?' she asked.

He looked about him, fearful that she might suddenly call out and bring the Britons down on him.

'Can we talk somewhere else?' he pleaded. 'Somewhere we can't be overheard.' He gestured at the crowd sitting around the nearby campfire, and whispered: 'I promise I mean you no harm. I will not attack you.'

'No, you will not,' Aithne told him firmly. 'If you did, I would defeat you. I am my father's daughter. He is a warrior chief and has taught me fighting ways. You would be no match for me.' She regarded him closely. 'Do you have a weapon? A knife?'

'No.'

She nodded. 'Very well, we shall find somewhere private to talk.'

She led the way towards a clearing out of the light of the campfire.

'I could be lying,' said Castus as he walked with her.

'No,' said Aithne, shaking her head. 'I know when people are lying and when they are telling the truth.'

'Is that a magic power from being a Wise Woman?' asked Castus.

* * *

Aithne nearly laughed out loud at Caradoc's nervousness as he asked about her Wise Woman powers. She was tempted to tell him that there was no magic, that it was all about observation, but she wasn't sure he would understand. And, for the moment, it would do no harm to keep him on edge, worried that she might really have some sort of magic powers. It would stop him from attempting to run away from her.

'We will talk here,' said Aithne, choosing a spot away from everyone. 'Now, why are you here?'

'The Governor sent me.'

'As he sent you to Mona?' asked Aithne.

He nodded, his face miserable.

'Yes,' he said. 'But this is different.'

'How?'

'When I went to Mona, I believed what I'd been told about the Britons. That they – you – were little more than animals. I didn't know any different. I'd spent my whole life with the Roman army.'

'But you look like a Briton,' said Aithne.

'My mother was a Briton,' said the boy.

'And your father?'

'He was a Roman soldier. He used to tell me that not all Britons were bad. He loved my mother. But, after he was killed in battle, I was brought up by another Roman soldier and his wife, and they had a very different attitude towards Britons.'

'They said we were animals,' said Aithne. 'Uncivilized barbarians.'

'Yes,' he admitted. 'So, when the Governor ordered me to go to Mona to spy on the forces and encampments of the Britons, I was proud to do it. But then ... ' He faltered, then finished: 'I saw things differently. Yes, some of the Britons wanted me put to death because they thought I was a spy ... '

'But you were saved by my father,' said Aithne. 'He spoke up for you.' She looked at him accusingly. 'You tricked him.'

'You told him so?' he asked.

Aithne shook her head.

'No,' she said. 'What good would it have done then? But now it's different. You betrayed him, and all of us.'

'No!' the boy burst out. 'Yes, I was sent to spy, but on the island I saw the Britons up close for the first time, saw the families with their children, where before I'd only seen warrior Britons in battle with our Roman soldiers.'

'But you still betrayed us,' said Aithne.

'No. The invasion took place before I could make my report,' said the boy. 'The Governor didn't wait. Perhaps he'd heard about Boudicca's uprising and decided he had to make his move.'

'But you would have reported to him!' accused Aithne.

The boy dropped his head.

'That was my mission,' he admitted in a small voice. 'But the invasion was coming anyway. There was nothing I could do to stop it.'

'And here you are, spying again so that we will all die.'

'The Governor thought the ruse had worked before, on Mona, so he sent me to join Boudicca's army. He sent me with his advance force.'

'What advance force?' asked Aithne, frowning.

'Suetonius knew it would take a long time for his army to reach Londinium, so he sent an advance force, lightly supplied so they could travel fast,' the boy replied. 'They were told to contain the rebellion until the main force of the army arrived. But when they neared Londinium they discovered just how big the rebellion was. Hundreds of thousands. A huge army. We met some of the soldiers who'd managed to escape from the slaughter at Camulodonum and they told us about it. So word was sent to Suetonius, and he ordered the advance force to abandon Londinium and head north to rejoin him.'

'He realized that they would be overwhelmed if they tried to defend Londinium, so he pulled them back to ensure he had a large force with him,' said Aithne.

The boy nodded.

'Where are they?' asked Aithne.

'I don't know,' he replied. 'They left me here with orders to join Boudicca's army when it arrived. Infiltrate it. I'm supposed to leave as soon as I can and head north to meet up with them and tell Suetonius what I've learned.'

'He has with him the same Roman soldiers who carried out the slaughter on Mona?'

He nodded.

'Soldiers who killed those women and children you talked about so caringly,' said Aithne bitterly.

'I didn't know they would kill everyone!' he insisted. 'I thought it would just be a battle with the warriors.'

'That's what you tell yourself, but you know in your heart the Roman aim is complete domination. They kill everyone who opposes them – men, women and children – to warn anyone else who might be thinking of doing the same. You knew they planned to kill everyone on the island.'

'No! I thought it would be warrior against warrior!' He looked appealingly at her. 'I'm not going back to the Romans,' he said. 'Not now I've seen what the Britons are really like. People, like us.'

'No, not like *you*,' said Aithne. 'You are a Roman. Romans slaughter without mercy.'

'So does Boudicca's army,' he protested. 'I have heard them boasting of killing ordinary civilians.' He shook his head, then added, 'But I met others on my way here who have been kind and gentle. And there are just as many decent soldiers as there are ruthless killers. I won't betray them.'

'So what will you do?' asked Aithne.

He looked at her, helplessness in his face.

'I don't know,' he said. 'I want to run away, but to where? Sooner or later people will discover I'm not really a Briton, just as you've done. But I can't go back to the Romans. I no longer believe in what they're doing. This endless slaughter.'

'I will keep your secret,' Aithne told him. 'Except for one person: I have to tell my father.'

'No!' the boy exclaimed. 'He is a warrior. He will kill me!'

'I will not lie to my father,' said Aithne. 'He is a good and honest man.'

'He will still kill me,' the boy insisted. 'For what happened on Mona.'

'If I'm to keep your secret, then you have to trust me,' said Aithne. 'My father trusts me. If I ask him to keep your secret, he will. He may not like doing it, but he will.'

The boy hesitated, then nodded.

'I'm putting my life in your hands,' he said reluctantly, 'but I feel I can trust you. I hope I'm not wrong.'

'I hope I'm not wrong about you,' said Aithne.

'I will prove I trust you,' the boy said. 'I will tell you my real name. My Roman name. With that, you could condemn me to death.'

Aithne shook her head.

'No,' she said. 'If you are to truly escape and be free, you must forget that name. From this day forward, you are Caradoc.'

Chapter 11
The Truth

Caradoc followed Aithne to find her father. The whole way there, his body jangled with nerves. She was going to tell Drustan about him! Caradoc was sure he would be killed: it was what the Romans would do if they discovered a British spy in their camp. And he knew, from what the chiefs had said about him on Mona, that the Britons felt the same way about spies.

I should run! he told himself. But where to? He would be easily caught. It was hopeless either way.

They arrived at the campfire where Aithne's father sat talking with his friends. Caradoc recognized him as one of the chiefs who'd been at the Council meeting on Mona. He was the warrior who'd spoken up for him, just as Aithne said. How would he react when Aithne told her father the truth about him? The man would kill him. The sight of the longsword that Drustan carried made Caradoc feel sick.

'Wait here,' said Aithne. 'I'll talk to my father away from his friends, and then bring him to talk to you.'

'He will hate me,' groaned Caradoc.

'Yes, at first he will,' agreed Aithne. 'But he will listen to me.'

Caradoc moved to a tree out of the light of the campfire and sat down on a stump. He watched as Aithne strode towards her father.

Run, you fool! he urged himself. *This is your last chance if you want to live!*

* * *

Drustan got to his feet as he saw Aithne arrive.

'You are safe!' he exclaimed. 'I had my fears when Nova said she needed to talk to you privately. I was tempted to refuse. She is ruthless and untrustworthy.'

'You remember her?' asked Aithne.

'I do,' nodded Drustan. 'I remember she was jealous of you when you were small. She would play spiteful tricks on you. Now, I'm guessing, she uses her spite to – ' He stopped, and, taking Aithne's arm, moved her out of earshot of the others around the fire. 'Nova encourages the Queen to be cruel. Boudicca was never this harsh before. Not to civilians. Garth and Trey say she changed after the Romans took her prisoner, and that may be true. But it is as if the good side of her has been eaten away by the bad side. Now there's only hatred and a thirst for revenge against anyone who's not completely on her side, whether they're a Roman or a Briton. It's just like the men on the road said. British bakers who sold bread to Romans were killed, and their shops burned to the ground. Butchers who sold meat to the Romans suffer the same fate.

'But they have to sell their wares to feed and clothe their families. They can't afford to refuse to sell to people because they are Roman, or from another tribe who've surrendered to the Romans. Has Boudicca forgotten that her own husband surrendered our tribe to the Romans? And she enjoyed all the comforts of a luxurious life under the Romans, until Prasutagus died.'

'By all accounts, she was treated badly by the Romans when she was in prison,' Aithne reminded him. 'That changes a person.'

Drustan shook his head, unhappy. 'I want to drive the Romans out as much as anyone, but this isn't the way I want to fight wars. I won't kill our own people. I won't kill Britons.' He hesitated then added awkwardly: 'Except those who fought with the Romans against us.'

'So what will you do?' asked Aithne.

'I don't know,' Drustan admitted. 'Part of me says we should leave Boudicca to her own ways, while I find others who feel as I do: a band of warriors who will fight the Romans, but in an honourable way.'

'Men like Garth and Trey?'

Drustan shrugged. 'Possibly. Their first loyalty is to the Iceni, which means they've given their word to the Queen. I won't ask them to break their oath to her.'

'So it will be you and I,' said Aithne doubtfully. 'We would be a very small resistance.'

'With just a few others, we could use the tactics we've used before,' said Drustan. 'Surprise attacks by a small group of warriors. Inflict damage and then disappear. We know the lands, the marshes, the rivers and valleys, better than the Romans do.'

'It might work,' said Aithne. 'If you had others with you.' She looked at the multitudes of people thronging around the campfires, or sitting on their wagons. 'But I doubt if you'll find any here who'd join with you. And it will be dangerous to ask. You said yourself: Boudicca is suspicious of anyone who isn't completely on her side.'

'You're right,' nodded Drustan. 'For the moment, we will keep it to ourselves. But, when the time is right, we'll find our own way.'

'Meanwhile, there is another problem,' said Aithne. 'Do you remember the boy who was pulled from the sea on Mona?'

'Of course,' said Drustan. 'The runaway slave.'

'He's here,' said Aithne.

Drustan looked at her, astonishment on his face.

'Here?' he repeated. 'But ... how? How did he escape the slaughter?'

'Because he was a Roman spy.'

Drustan's face turned into a fierce mask of fury, his hand on the hilt of his sword.

'Show me where he is!' he grated. 'I'll kill him!'

'No,' said Aithne. 'He no longer works for the Romans.'

'That means nothing! He betrayed us.'

Aithne shook her head.

'He never made the report. He is just a boy, my age. He thought he was Roman, but now he wants to be a Briton. But the truth is, he'll never be either, the way things are. He's like a lost lamb. He needs someone to guide him.'

'You?' asked Drustan.

'Us,' said Aithne.

Drustan shook his head. 'I can't trust him,' he said. 'Not after what he did to us on Mona. He *lied*. He lied to the Council, he lied to us. He will lie again.'

'No,' insisted Aithne. 'He told me the truth about himself. He confessed. He won't lie to us again.'

Because he believes I have magic powers that can see what is really in his heart, she admitted to herself. But she wasn't going to tell her father that.

Drustan fell silent, lost in deep thought. Then he said: 'I don't like him. I *won't* like him.'

'You don't have to like him. But at the moment he's a lost boy who needs protecting.' Thoughtfully, she added, 'And, if we do what you are thinking of, abandoning Boudicca and striking out on our own, it might be useful to have someone with us who knows how the Roman army operates. It might save us from walking into dangerous situations.'

Drustan nodded.

'Now that is clever thinking, little one,' he said.

Clever, but not what I feel, thought Aithne. *Caradoc wants to take the right path, and to do that he needs our help.* But he wouldn't get it from her father while Drustan despised him as a spy. The warrior in Drustan now saw that Caradoc could be useful strategically. But Aithne knew that Caradoc would only be truly safe if Drustan could learn to trust him.

Chapter 12
Roman or Briton?

Caradoc got up from the tree stump where he was sitting as Aithne and Drustan approached. Aithne could see that he was trembling.

'My daughter tells me you are a spy,' growled Drustan.

'No!' Caradoc appealed to him. 'I was, but no longer!'

'Then why are you here?' demanded Drustan.

'I was *sent* as a spy – but I can't work for the Romans any more,' said Caradoc. He looked miserable. 'I don't know where to go or what to do.'

Drustan glowered at the boy. 'Everyone on Mona was killed,' he told him. 'You were with the Romans, so you were part of that. If Aithne hadn't spoken up for you, you would be dead already.'

Caradoc didn't answer, just hung his head, unable to look Drustan in the face.

'Where do you sleep?' asked Drustan.

'Anywhere,' shrugged Caradoc. 'I don't know people here. I only arrived yesterday, and I've been wary of talking to people I don't know.'

'You will sleep in our camp, with our friends,' Drustan told him. 'Tomorrow, Boudicca sets out northwards. Aithne will be joining her in her wagon, so you'll be in my care. If I suspect you of playing false, I will kill you.'

'I promise you, I will not play you false,' Caradoc whispered.

'What will you tell Garth and Trey?' asked Aithne.

'That he is an orphan we've taken under our wing,' said Drustan. He grunted. 'That much, at least, is true.'

'It is,' nodded Caradoc.

'In that case, follow us,' commanded Drustan. 'But be warned, I'm doing this for my daughter. I don't like you and I don't trust you.'

With that, Drustan headed towards the wagon where Garth and Trey were preparing to sleep.

Aithne smiled at Caradoc.

'See?' she said. 'He didn't kill you.'

Not yet, thought Caradoc miserably as he joined her, following Drustan.

* * *

That night, after Aithne and Drustan had climbed into the wagon to sleep, Caradoc reclined against one of the wagon's wheels, his mind a whirl. What should he do? He felt he could trust Aithne, but her father was another matter. He could sense the man's anger and loathing, and he knew for sure that if Aithne hadn't been present, Drustan would have struck him down there and then. His brain told him to flee – escape while he still could. But go where?

Caradoc was disenchanted with the Romans. He'd seen how the Britons lived, and how the Romans lived, and there was a warmth about some of the Britons that had been lacking for him in the Roman camp. The Roman army was built on a foundation of harsh discipline. If there were rumours of discontent in the ranks, soldiers grumbling about poor food or conditions, then it was suppressed immediately to stop it spreading. If the grumbling among a particular legion looked as if it might lead to open rebellion among the soldiers, then the commander would order decimation of that legion: the execution of every tenth soldier. It didn't matter whether the soldiers who died had been the real grumblers or troublemakers. The soldiers were lined up and every tenth man was killed. It was harsh but it certainly stopped people expressing discontent. That was why the Roman army had been so successful for so long and had conquered most of the world; because the soldiers were more afraid of their commanders than they were of any enemy. No Roman soldier would ever refuse or disobey an order. To do so would mean instant death – not just for the man who disobeyed, but for many of his fellow soldiers too.

The Britons were far less disciplined and organized, Caradoc thought. They seemed more interested in friendship and loyalty to each other than in serving some distant authority. And yet this ramshackle mob had defeated the Romans at Camulodonum.

As he sat with his back against the wheel, looking at the Britons laughing and playing while others slept, Caradoc realized that the overall feeling here was joy, as opposed to the feeling of fear that dominated the Roman way. The only person who seemed afraid was him.

Chapter 13
War Council

The next morning, Aithne left her father, Garth, Trey and Caradoc and made for Boudicca's wagon. All around her as she walked, people were packing their wagons ready to set off on their long journey. Again it struck Aithne that such a large number of them were women and children, brought along to watch as Boudicca's army continued its victorious march. There were many warriors, true, but there were also inexperienced men who'd dressed up as warriors, and equipped themselves with a sword or a staff, to impress the families they'd brought with them. How would they react when they came up against the might of the Roman army? Her father had passed on to her what Garth had told him: that most of the victories so far had been against old soldiers working out their retirement. What would happen when they faced the *real* Roman army, the mighty force which had attacked Mona?

Last night, out of earshot of Garth and Trey, Drustan had questioned Caradoc about the size of Suetonius's army.

'Ten thousand,' Caradoc had told them. 'The five thousand men he had with him at Mona, and another five thousand he's summoned from other camps.'

Ten thousand against Boudicca's army of a quarter of a million. But it was Aithne's guess that only about thirty thousand of that quarter of a million were proper hardened warriors, like her father and Garth and Trey. Thirty thousand against ten thousand was still in their favour, but the untrained warriors and the women and children worried her. They would get in the way.

Aithne arrived at Boudicca's wagon to find the Queen preparing for battle. Aithne noticed that – unlike her warriors who went into battle almost naked – she'd put on armour, a metal breast plate.

'Aithne!' Boudicca greeted her. 'You are just in time. I am taking counsel. I sent scouts out and they have reported back that Suetonius's army is just two days' march north from here. What strategies should we employ when we meet them? The same technique as before: a mass attack, as we did at Camulodonum? It worked then – the Romans ran like scared rabbits.' Her lips curled in a sneer as she added: 'Although I have heard that some people are saying the enemy we faced then were old and decrepit.'

'Lies!' spat Nova, stepping forward from the cover of the wagon, and Aithne saw that Boudicca had assembled her Wise Women, four of them, along with two Druids. 'Your victories were against the might of the all-powerful Roman army, my Queen. Anyone who tries to belittle those triumphs is a traitor. We must seek out those who say such things and make an example of them before the treasonous words of these cowards undermine the true warriors who are with us!'

'Thank you, Nova,' smiled Boudicca. She turned her piercing look towards Aithne. 'Have you heard this being said? Do you know who is spreading these lies?'

'No, my Queen,' replied Aithne. 'But then, I only arrived last night.'

'Yes, from Mona, where you saw Suetonius's army up close,' nodded Boudicca. 'What is your impression of them? How many soldiers did he have?'

'About five thousand,' said Aithne.

'Five thousand!' smirked Nova. 'Against this army of ours! We will crush them!'

'He may have gathered more,' said Aithne, remembering what Caradoc had said.

'But not too many more,' said Boudicca. 'I believe that most of his forces are in the south-west. But do you agree, Aithne? Will we crush them?'

I have to be careful, thought Aithne. *Boudicca reads people, just as I do. But she has changed since all this began. She now pays heed to flatterers, like Nova, and their praise clouds her judgement.*

'Yes, my Queen,' nodded Aithne. 'If the warriors are given space to manoeuvre.'

Boudicca frowned. 'What do you mean?' she demanded.

'I believe the wagons with the women and children should be kept away from the battle,' said Aithne. 'They will get in the way when our warriors attack.'

'No!' cried Nova. She turned to Boudicca. 'The families with the women and children should be at the front! The Romans will tire quicker if they have to attack them first, giving our warriors an advantage. And the women and children will cause havoc among the Romans.'

Was Nova offering the deaths of women and children as a way of achieving victory? Aithne found it hard to hide her anger, but she had to. Nova was a dangerous enemy.

'The Romans didn't tire when they killed the women and children on Mona,' said Aithne carefully.

'That was because there was just a handful of them,' countered Nova. She gestured at the wagons and people milling around. 'Look at them! Thousands and thousands of people ready to die for our Queen as we drive the Romans out! Five thousand Romans against an army of this size? They won't stand a chance!'

'You see how valuable Nova has become to me, Aithne?' said Boudicca. 'She thinks like a warrior. However, I believe our best course of action would be to combine the advice you both give. We will put our best warriors at the front, but we will bring the wagons in close

behind them so the women will act as a further line
of defence.'

Boudicca's servants slipped the Queen's cloak over her
shoulders and held it in place with a gold torc. Boudicca
took a spear from where it was resting against her wagon
and hefted it in her hand.

'We are ready!' she announced. 'Let us go forth and
face these Romans, and humiliate them so thoroughly that
no Roman will ever show his face in Britannia again.'

Chapter 14
An Army on the Move

With such a massive army, most of them foot-soldiers or hangers-on, the pace was slow. Boudicca headed the procession, riding in a chariot drawn by two horses. On the chariot with her was the driver, and Nova.

Aithne was on the wagon immediately behind Boudicca's chariot, along with a Seer and three other Wise Women. She watched Nova: there was a smug smirk of triumph on her face as she turned this way and that, as if to say, *See! I am at the right hand of the Queen! I am the most important person in her court! Look at me and fear me, for I am powerful!*

Aithne remembered that Nova had always been ambitious, but in this she had exceeded her dreams. To be at the head of an army of a quarter of a million people, alongside the Queen!

Why am I here? thought Aithne. *The Queen has no use for my counsel. Nova will make sure of that.*

Yes, Boudicca had sent the feather, summoning her. But that had been before her latest triumphs, before her victories. Now, nothing that Aithne could say would change Boudicca's determination to fight the Romans in her own way. And why should she change when she had been victorious so far?

But victorious against retired soldiers. The army that Aithne had seen assembling by the barges at Mona had been a fighting machine.

Yet perhaps, as Nova had said, this fighting machine would find themselves overwhelmed by the vast waves of Britons – men, women and children – who were ready to hurl themselves at the Romans. Aithne turned and looked behind her. The column filled the whole width of the road: wagons, people on foot, spears and banners held proudly aloft. An army on the march.

I wonder how my father is getting on with Caradoc, she thought.

* * *

Caradoc sat in the back of the wagon as it trundled along, hemmed in by walking Britons and other carts and wagons. The two Iceni warriors, Garth and Trey, sat at the front, driving the horses. Drustan sat in the back with Caradoc, his angry glowering eyes fixed on the boy.

He hates me, Caradoc thought miserably. *He hates all Romans.*

But I am not completely Roman. Yes, in my heart and in my head I was, at the time Suetonius summoned me and gave me his orders, but if my father had been alive it would have been different. He would have let me be half-Briton, half-Roman.

He looked about him at the mob surrounding their cart, all heading northwards, eager to attack the Romans, and thought: *But I am not like them, either. If anything, I am like the girl, Aithne. She has no love for what is happening here. I will follow her advice. She told me I must forget my Roman name.*

Yes, he told himself. *From now on I will be Caradoc, and not just in name. I will be my mother's son, a Briton.*

Chapter 15
Goodbye

Boudicca called the column to a halt after a few hours to give the horses and those on foot a chance to rest. As fires were lit to cook food, Aithne decided to go to find her father, worried that there might be trouble between him and Caradoc. She was just heading off into the mass of people, when she found Nova barring her way.

'Where are you going?' demanded Nova icily.

'To talk to my father,' said Aithne.

'About what?' snapped Nova.

'To reassure him that I am safe and well and happy to be reunited with the Queen once more,' replied Aithne. 'He worries about me.'

Nova scowled. 'Let us hope he doesn't run away when the battle begins, as he did against the Romans on Mona.'

A feeling of rage filled Aithne at these words, and she had to stop herself from slapping Nova.

'My father only left Mona because we were summoned by the Queen! My father was always the most courageous warrior of the Iceni, the one who fought against the Romans the hardest, which is why he had to leave when the King surrendered our tribe to them. He fought them all the way to Mona, while others of the Iceni stayed and curried favour with them!'

'*I* never curried favour with the Romans!' Nova snarled. 'And as for the Queen summoning you, that was before she realized that, with me at her side, she had no need of you.'

'Then perhaps I should tell the Queen what you have said, and ask if she wants me to leave her service,' Aithne replied.

Nova hesitated, caught out by Aithne's challenge. Then she snapped: 'You will *not* talk to the Queen about what we have said just now. You can go to your father, but you will return. The Queen still seems to want you around.' She sniffed. 'I expect she feels pity for you. You once showed promise as a Wise Woman.'

Aithne hurried off, aware of Nova's malevolent glare aimed at her back.

I must watch myself with her, she warned herself again. *I mustn't let my anger at her make me say things she can use against me.*

When Aithne arrived at Garth and Trey's wagon, she saw Caradoc sitting unhappily on his own, while Drustan, Garth and Trey sat by a fire, roasting small bits of meat on sticks. Caradoc got to his feet when he saw Aithne, and looked as if he was going to hurry towards her, but he stopped himself when he saw Drustan rise and head for her.

'What has happened?' asked Aithne. 'Why is Caradoc on his own?'

'I put him there,' grunted Drustan.

'Why?'

'Because I can't stand the sight of him,' growled Drustan. 'I cannot do this, Aithne. I cannot let him be here with us, knowing what he is.'

'What he *was*,' Aithne corrected him.

'Are you so sure he's changed?' demanded Drustan. 'He's a *Roman*.'

'He's half-Briton.'

'So he claims,' muttered her father.

'You said yourself, he looks like a Briton,' Aithne pointed out.

'Yes, all right, perhaps his mother was a Briton,' conceded Drustan reluctantly. 'But I must tell Garth and Trey the truth about him, otherwise I'm lying to warriors I've fought side by side with – men who trust me!'

Aithne shook her head. 'They wouldn't understand,' she said.

'*I* don't understand!' exploded her father. Garth, Trey and Caradoc all looked towards them. He lowered his voice to a whisper as he added, 'He has to go away.'

'Where to?' demanded Aithne.

'I don't care. Back to his Roman masters. He can wander the countryside. But I cannot endure his presence!'

'He's just a boy,' Aithne appealed.

'When I was his age I had already fought in battles against the tribes who invaded our territory,' countered Drustan.

'He is not a warrior,' said Aithne. 'You can see that. He is a servant. He won't survive on his own.'

'Then it's time he learned.'

Aithne sighed. 'Very well. Will you tell him he has to go, or shall I?'

'I will,' said Drustan. 'It will be easier for me than for you. I don't want him around when we go into battle. When that happens it will be warrior against Roman soldier, and I can't afford to have half my attention on what he's up to.'

'The Queen is going to order that the wagons with the women and children be brought in close to the action,' said Aithne. 'They are to be a last line of defence.'

Drustan shook his head disapprovingly. 'Women and children will be no match for these Roman soldiers,' he said. 'It will be a slaughter if the Romans reach them, just as it was on Mona.'

'The idea came from Nova,' said Aithne. 'She originally wanted the wagons at the front, to create chaos among the Romans. This is Boudicca's compromise. Other tribes have done the same, Father. Some put the women into the front line of battle.'

'Not the Iceni,' said Drustan. 'It is not our way.'

'Boudicca is a woman and an Iceni warrior,' pointed out Aithne. 'She is on the front line.'

'Boudicca is different,' grunted Drustan. 'She is our Queen.'

There is no use arguing with him, thought Aithne. She looked across to where Caradoc was sitting, watching them. 'When will you talk to Caradoc?'

'Later,' replied Drustan. 'First I need to talk to Garth and Trey.'

He headed back towards the campfire and his fellow warriors. Caradoc immediately got to his feet and hurried to join Aithne.

'Your father wants me to go,' he said.

'You heard him?' asked Aithne, surprised.

'I didn't need to hear what he said, I could tell by watching you and him. Remember, I've been brought up by the Romans, who are a hard people with harsh discipline. You can get a whipping for almost anything, which means I learned to be on my guard and watch those around me, to spot if there might be trouble coming my way. I could tell he was talking about me – he glared in my direction now and then, and I could tell you were trying to calm him down. But I could see from his face and the way he walked away that you didn't succeed this time.'

Aithne nodded sadly. 'I'm sorry,' she said.

'At least he hasn't told the others about me.'

'What will you do?' asked Aithne.

'I don't know,' admitted Caradoc. 'I don't want to go back to the Romans, but I won't be able to survive for long among the Britons. Sooner or later I'll say something that gives away who I really am. But I have to go. If I stay, your father won't be able to stop himself saying something.'

'When will you go?'

'Tonight,' said Caradoc. He forced a smile. 'And thank you.'

'For what?' asked Aithne. 'It was because I told my father about you that you have to leave.'

'You cared for me on Mona. You took care of me again when you arrived here. You could have betrayed me and gained credit with Boudicca, but you didn't. I think you are the kindest person I've ever met. After my mother and father.' He held out his hand for her to shake. As she took it, he added: 'I hope you and your father survive.'

Chapter 16
Captured

A sense of despair filled Aithne as she headed back to Boudicca's wagon. She should never have told Drustan the truth about Caradoc. By doing so, she'd put her father in an impossible position, torn between his love for her and loyalty to his closest warrior friends. And, as a result, the boy would roam loose, unable to settle with either side, until he met his fate: at the hands of the Romans, or angry Britons.

Hardly a 'Wise Woman', she told herself bitterly.

She was almost at Boudicca's wagon, when she heard her father's voice calling: 'Aithne! Wait!'

She turned and saw Drustan hurrying towards her.

'I went to tell the boy he had to leave, but he said you'd already spoken to him,' he said when he reached her.

'He guessed what we were saying, from watching us talk,' explained Aithne.

Drustan nodded. 'It will be for the best,' he said.

'You think so?'

'What I think about the boy doesn't matter any more,' said Drustan. 'I've decided I've got to leave, and I want you to come with me.'

'Leave?' echoed Aithne.

'I've been thinking about what you told me. The families and the women and children in the wagons being put so close to the action. Warriors need space to move when in battle. Sometimes they need to pull back before they can attack again.' He shook his head. 'We will be fighting hardened soldiers this time. This so-called strategy of bringing the wagons close is foolish. And this ramshackle army ... If we are ever to defeat the Romans completely we must build a proper force of warriors. So I shall do what I said I would: join up with others who feel the same way as I do, and mount raids against the Romans, warrior against warrior.'

'So you accuse the Queen of foolishness and would desert her cause,' said a voice.

They turned, startled, and saw Nova appear from the cover of the wagon. With her were six warriors, their spears pointed directly at Drustan and Aithne. Automatically, Drustan's hand dropped to his sword.

'Touch it and she dies first,' said Nova, pointing at Aithne. She smiled. 'I don't think you'd like to see your precious daughter speared.'

Drustan removed his hand from his sword hilt.

'I knew something was wrong,' smirked Nova. 'I've been following you, Aithne, waiting for you or your father to reveal yourselves as the traitors I know you are.'

'We are not traitors,' declared Aithne defiantly.

'No? The Queen can judge exactly how loyal you are, once she's heard what you were saying about deserting,' said Nova. 'And it will not be just my word against yours.' She indicated the six armed men with her. 'We all heard what you said, Drustan. That so far we've only fought old Roman soldiers put out to grass. You called our own Queen's strategy foolish.'

'Those were my words, not Aithne's,' said Drustan. 'Aithne has no part in this.'

'Oh, I think she has,' said Nova. She gave them a nasty smile of triumph. 'But we'll let the Queen decide.'

* * *

Boudicca sat on the fur-covered chair she used as a throne while travelling, and fixed Aithne and Drustan with a hard glare.

'So you would betray me?' she growled.

'I would never betray you, my Queen ... ' began Drustan.

He was cut short by Boudicca's angry shout: 'You will be silent!'

Aithne looked at Nova, who was standing with Bex and Riana, a smug smirk on her face. Four of the armed guards had stayed outside the wagon, and two stood close to Drustan and Aithne. Drustan's sword and knife had been taken from him.

'I never thought I would see the day when my own warrior, Drustan, would abandon me.' Boudicca shook her head. 'The only punishment there can be is death. I will have you executed in front of the whole tribe, as an example to anyone else thinking of following your treacherous example.'

Nova stepped forward to the Queen and whispered something in her ear. Boudicca let her words sink in, then nodded.

'A good thought, Nova. You are wise.' To Drustan and Aithne, she said: 'For the moment, your lives will be spared.' She turned to the guards and commanded: 'Take them and put them in a covered wagon, I don't want anyone looking upon them. And make sure they are bound by the wrists and ankles, and tied firmly to the struts of the wagon. If they escape, you will die in their place.'

* * *

Caradoc stood at the back of the crowd and watched as Aithne and Drustan were pushed towards a covered wagon by armed men. Around him, angry murmurs had already broken out, mutterings of 'traitors' and 'treason'. Someone called out, 'Kill them!'

What had happened? Had Boudicca somehow found out about him? Were Aithne and Drustan being punished for protecting him?

'What's happened?' he asked the man next to him. 'What have they done?'

'They were going to run away and desert us,' growled the man.

'What will they do to them?' asked Caradoc.

'Kill them, of course!' said the man. 'They are traitors.' He shook his head. 'I don't know why they don't kill them here and now and get it over with. I suppose it's because of who they are: he's supposed to be a great Iceni warrior, and she's one of Boudicca's own Wise Women. I expect Boudicca's got something special in mind for them. But they'll die, that's for sure.'

Chapter 17
Trapped

Caradoc was just about to head back to Garth and Trey's campfire when he saw the two Iceni warriors standing at the back of the crowd, dark scowls on both their faces. Caradoc hurried towards them.

'Did you see?' he demanded urgently. 'Drustan and Aithne have been taken prisoner!'

Garth nodded, his face grim. 'We saw.'

'But why?' asked Caradoc, still dumbfounded by this turn of events.

'They say Drustan was going to desert,' said Garth. 'And take Aithne with him.'

'Treason,' nodded Trey.

'Surely you don't believe that!' Caradoc appealed to them. 'You know them. You fought alongside Drustan, you know he is no traitor.'

'And how well do you know him, boy?' asked Garth suspiciously. 'They said they found you here, a lost orphan, and took you in. But I get the feeling you know them better than that, for some reason.'

'No,' said Caradoc, shaking his head. 'It's just that I'm grateful for them taking me in, the way they did. No one's ever been kind to me like that before. I feel I owe them. Someone must speak up for them.'

'You?' queried Trey.

'No one would listen to me,' groaned Caradoc. 'I'm just an abandoned orphan. But you are warriors of the Iceni, who fought alongside Drustan. You know them. Boudicca will listen to you!'

Garth shook his head. 'We have sworn an oath of allegiance to our Queen,' he said. 'We cannot break it.'

'But they will be killed!' Caradoc implored them.

'Drustan has been away too long,' said Trey. 'Things change.'

'But not his oath of allegiance,' added Garth. 'He swore to defend the King and Queen. If what I hear is true and he decided to abandon Boudicca, he has broken his oath.'

Trey turned to face Caradoc and looked intently into his eyes. 'My advice to you, boy, is to be careful what you say,' he warned. 'It wouldn't do for you to speak up for them to anyone else here; you'll just find yourself in the same fix.'

'If you're lucky,' added Garth. 'Drustan is a powerful warrior, and Aithne is a Wise Woman. They're only alive because Boudicca has something big in mind for them later. You said yourself, you're just a boy without a family. Boudicca will have you killed as soon as look at you.'

Chapter 18

Rescue

The army marched on, always northwards, following Boudicca in her warrior's chariot. Caradoc joined those travelling on foot, keeping his distance from the covered wagon where Aithne and Drustan were being kept, but making sure he had it in sight. The initial anger among the crowd towards them had died down. People were more concerned about the forthcoming battle with the Romans. The Final Battle, that was how everyone was describing it. The battle that would see the Romans crushed and driven out of Britannia.

The wagon in which Aithne and Drustan were kept seemed to be very lightly guarded, just the driver at the front and one man with a spear walking behind. Caradoc guessed that they must be securely tied inside the wagon for there to be so little thought given to guarding them.

As darkness fell, the army pulled to a halt. The wagon containing Aithne and Drustan was abandoned by the driver, and another man armed with a spear and a sword took over guard duty at the rear, freeing the one who'd walked behind the wagon to go and join his companions by a fire, to eat and drink.

Only one guard, reflected Caradoc. If they had been prisoners in a Roman camp there would have been at least four soldiers, all heavily armed, detailed to keep watch over them. But, as he'd noticed before, the Britons didn't seem so strong on discipline.

The man with the spear sat down on the steps of the wagon and slumped back, giving a yawn. Again, if he'd been a Roman on guard, he would have had to stand to attention, remain alert.

Ever since he'd seen Aithne and Drustan taken into the covered wagon, Caradoc had debated his course of action. Should he do what he'd told Aithne he was going to – sneak away once darkness fell and people were asleep – or try and rescue them?

The first would keep him alive, at least for a while. But if he did run away, he knew he had no choice other than to head north and meet up with the oncoming Romans, and become one of them again.

Yet he knew he couldn't stay with Boudicca's army, not now Aithne and Drustan had been taken prisoner. He was at risk of sharing their fate, if anyone remembered seeing him in close conversation with them. Sooner or later someone would accuse him of being in league with them, and then the awkward questions would start. Where had he come from? What was his tribe? Who could vouch for him?

No one could vouch for him. That was the stark truth.

He had to leave. But he couldn't desert Aithne and Drustan. They had shown him kindness – well, Aithne had – and he owed them his life. With one word they could have exposed him and sentenced him to death, but they chose to protect him. And now, they were facing death themselves.

He fingered the knife he'd taken from Garth's wagon, which was now hidden inside his tunic. It was Drustan's knife, which had been given to Trey and Garth by one of the Wise Women, along with Drustan's sword, with orders for the weapons of the traitor to be burned. But Caradoc had found the knife and kept it.

His plan was to creep into the wagon and free Aithne and Drustan. Then they could escape together. The question was: when should he make his move? Now, while everyone was busy settling down and making fires – or later, once people went to sleep? But with people asleep, any movements in the camp would be noticed. And what if more guards came to keep watch on the prisoners? Or if the wagon driver returned?

Once more, he looked towards the wagon. The man with the spear who'd been sitting on the steps got to his feet as another armed man came to join him. They talked briefly, and then the later arrival went off. But would he come back?

I'll wait until later, Caradoc decided. He hoped that eventually the guard might drop off to sleep.

Then an awful thought struck him. Could it be that there was only one man on guard because Aithne and Drustan were no longer a danger to anyone? Because they were already dead, killed in the secrecy of the covered wagon?

A sudden fit of trembling overtook him. But it wasn't from cold. It was fear.

* * *

Most of the camp slept. Just a few people wandered around, moving from campfire to campfire. Caradoc sat and looked towards the covered wagon. The guard with the spear had definitely sagged on the steps. If he wasn't actually asleep, he was close to it, leaning back almost in a sprawl. There was no sign of the driver – the seat at the front of the wagon was empty.

One question worried Caradoc: was anyone in the wagon with Aithne and Drustan? He hadn't seen anyone enter the wagon, and he'd been watching it intently for hours, but that didn't mean that someone wasn't already in there, keeping a close guard on them.

That would be the case if they were prisoners of the Romans, but the Britons were more casual.

Caradoc got up and made for the front of the wagon,

walking slowly, casually, determined not to draw attention to his movements. He reached the wagon and leaned against it, running his hands over the wood of the driver's seat, on edge as he waited to see if anyone would call out telling him to leave the wagon alone.

No one did.

It's now or never, he told himself, his heart thumping so loudly that someone else must surely hear it beating. He took a last look around to make sure no one was watching, then pulled himself up on to the driver's seat.

He pulled out the knife and made a swift downward cut in the cloth behind the seat, then pushed through into the interior of the wagon.

In the darkness of the wagon he could just make out two shapes, one large, one small. He whispered: 'It's me, Caradoc. I've come to free you.'

He edged towards the nearest shape, and heard Drustan say, puzzled: 'The boy?'

'Ssssh!' said Caradoc urgently.

He used the knife to cut at the ropes that held the Iceni warrior to a wooden strut, and as they fell away he started work on those that bound the man's arms and legs.

As soon as he was free, Drustan hissed, 'Give me the knife! I can cut quicker than you!'

Drustan took the knife and set to work on the ropes that bound Aithne, and moments later she was free.

'There is a guard on the back steps,' Caradoc whispered. He indicated the cut he'd made at the front of the wagon. 'This way.'

He guided Aithne to the cut in the fabric, and she went through first, followed by Drustan. Then Caradoc pushed his head through. As he did so, he sensed rather than saw a movement to one side of him – then felt a colossal pain as something smashed down on his head, and everything went black.

Chapter 19
The Final Battle

Slowly, Caradoc came round. His head pounded: everything was pain. He went to touch his head, but found he couldn't. His hands were bound tightly together.

'It was a trap,' said Aithne's voice. 'They wanted to see if anyone would try and rescue us.'

'And they caught you,' said Drustan. 'I'm sorry.'

As Caradoc's eyes became accustomed to the dark in the wagon, he saw that all three of them were now tied up securely.

'It was Nova's idea,' said Aithne. 'In her words: to catch other traitors.'

'My head hurts,' groaned Caradoc.

'You were hit pretty hard,' said Drustan. 'I guess that they lay in wait for us once they'd seen you go in.'

'Still, they didn't kill us,' Caradoc managed to say.

'I think they're saving that pleasure until later today,' said Drustan sourly.

Caradoc became aware that the wagon was shaking, jerking them from side to side.

'We're moving,' he said.

'We've been moving for a while,' said Drustan.

'Nova came and told us that the Romans had been sighted a few miles ahead,' added Aithne. 'She said that after Boudicca's defeated them, we'll be killed to give thanks for her victory.'

'You shouldn't have tried to save us,' said Drustan. 'There was no need for you to die as well.'

'I owed you for the way you welcomed me,' said Caradoc.

Drustan shook his head.

'I didn't,' he admitted.

'Aithne did,' said Caradoc.

'I was wrong about you, boy,' said Drustan. 'You are loyal and brave. I will plead for your life with Boudicca.'

'She won't listen to you,' said Aithne sadly. 'Her ears are too full of Nova's words.'

'We're not dead yet,' said Caradoc, trying to force a confident tone. 'My father always said while there's life, there's hope. My real father, that is.'

'He was Roman?' asked Aithne.

'He was,' said Caradoc. 'My mother was from the Dobunni. They met while he was on duty in the Dobunni territory. They were together for a year before I was born, and they were so close I know they would still have been together today. She died soon after he was killed. Some of the other women in the camp said she died of a broken heart.'

'How did he die?' asked Drustan.

'He was in a scouting party which was ambushed by Britons.'

'When was this?'

'Three years ago. Wintertime. We were still in the Dobunni territory.'

Drustan fell silent, then said, 'I was in a raid that ambushed a Roman scouting party in the territory of the Dobunni, three years ago during winter. They fought bravely. We killed them all and lost four of our own.'

Caradoc looked at Drustan warily, then said: 'The soldiers who went in support of the scouting party found four dead Britons with them.'

'We had no time to take our fallen with us,' said Drustan. 'We heard more Romans coming, and by then there were just four of us left.' He looked at Caradoc, then said, 'It's possible that I killed your father.'

Caradoc nodded. 'It is war,' he said. 'At least, that's what my father used to say after a battle. He had no hatred for the Britons, or for anyone he fought. It was what he was trained to do.'

They fell silent, rocking with the movement of the wagon as it trundled along. Finally, it stopped. Outside they heard shouting and the sounds of activity.

'They are getting ready for the battle,' said Drustan. He scowled at the ropes that bound him. 'My knife is missing. I wish I could get free!'

'Like this?' asked Aithne, and she held up her hands as the ropes fell away.

Drustan and Caradoc stared at her, stunned.

'It's magic!' said Caradoc, awed. 'Wise Woman magic!'

Aithne shook her head. 'This time, when they tied my wrists, I held my hands pressed together in such a stiff way that, when I relaxed them, the ropes became loose. I've been working my hands backwards and forwards, up and down, to get out from the knots.' She reached down to the ropes that bound her ankles together and began to pick at the knots. 'Once I get free, I'll work on yours.'

'You are indeed a Wise Woman, Aithne,' said her father admiringly. 'The wisest of all!'

Aithne corrected him sadly: 'If I was the wisest of all, we wouldn't be in this trouble.'

* * *

The knots in the ropes around Aithne's ankles were much tighter and took much longer to unpick. All the time she kept her ears alert for anyone coming into the wagon, worried that her attempts to get free might be discovered. But, from the sounds she could hear outside, it seemed that everyone was too preoccupied with the coming battle to bother with them.

After what seemed like an eternity, Aithne was finally free, and she went immediately to Drustan and began to work at the knots that imprisoned him. Again, it was a long, laborious task.

By now, the sounds outside had become more distant: yells and cries, shrill shouting, the sound of metal crashing against metal.

'They have left us away from the action,' commented Drustan. 'I would guess the battle is happening at least a mile away from where we are.'

Aithne continued working at the ropes that bound Drustan's wrists, and finally they fell free. She left her father to work on the ropes that tied his ankles, while she turned her attention to Caradoc.

Finally, with her fingertips raw from the rough hempen ropes, the three of them were free.

'What now?' asked Caradoc.

'Now, we leave,' said Drustan. 'The only thing we can do is what I intended: get away from this chaotic mob and continue our rebellion against the Romans on our own.'

'That depends on whether there are any Romans left,' said Aithne.

She moved towards the slit in the wagon's covering to go out, but Drustan stopped her.

'I'll go first,' he said. 'In case any guards have been left here with us.'

He pushed his way out. Caradoc looked at Aithne.

'In case we are caught, and killed, I just want you to know that I'm glad I met you,' he said. 'I'm sorry I lied at first.'

'You did what you had to do,' said Aithne. 'I thank you for trying to rescue us. You didn't need to.'

The fabric at the front of the wagon parted, and Drustan looked in.

'You can come out,' he said. 'There's no one here.'

Chapter 20
Aftermath

They stood on the crest of a hill and looked towards the site of the battle. From this distance, more than a mile away, the people seemed as small as ants. It was obvious that the Romans had been victorious. The scene was one of devastation. The sun glinted on the armour of the soldiers as they moved through the remnants of Boudicca's army. Wagons and carts lay broken, with many of the fallen Britons caught on their wreckage.

'The Romans attacked and the Britons tried to run, but having the wagons and carts so close must have stopped them from getting away,' muttered Drustan. 'If it hadn't been for that, they could have regrouped, then attacked again. It happened just as I said it would.'

Aithne shook her head. 'It was more than just that. The Romans chose this site well to make their defence.' She pointed. 'See how narrow it is. A deep gorge, and uphill, with a thick forest at the back. The Roman position couldn't be surrounded, so it was the front line of the Romans against the front line of Boudicca's army. There was no hope of the Britons creeping round behind the Roman lines to spring a surprise attack.'

'And in that situation, the Romans would always win,'

added Caradoc. 'They're more disciplined and they're better armed ... ' His voice trailed off.

'It is over,' said Drustan heavily.

'The final battle,' nodded Caradoc.

'No,' said Drustan defiantly. 'This was not the final battle! There will be others! And next time, we will win!'

They fell silent, shocked by the destruction they could see before them.

'We should go,' said Aithne. 'The Romans will come to check these wagons.'

'Yes,' said Drustan. He turned to Caradoc. 'Three years ago, I robbed you of your father. Will you travel with us and allow me to be a father in his place?'

'I'd be honoured,' said Caradoc. He looked at Aithne, questioningly. 'What do you think?' he asked.

Aithne smiled. 'I have a brother!'

The three of them turned and headed away from the scene of the battle, on a quest to build new lives from the carnage they left behind. To build a new Britannia.

The history of *Warrior Queen*

Before the story

By 55 BCE the Romans had already conquered most of
mainland Europe, but they hadn't yet set foot in Britain.
In that year, Julius Caesar led a Roman invasion
of the country. A year later, he came again.

At this time Britain was divided into tribal areas, each
with its own king or queen. The King of southern Britain
agreed to pay a ransom to the Romans and in return they
left.

They didn't come back for almost a hundred years.
But in 43 CE, a Roman army arrived in Britain under
the command of the Emperor Claudius. This time, when
Claudius returned to Rome, he left behind troops to
enforce Roman rule.

Unsurprisingly, British tribes began to rebel against
the Romans.

In 60 CE Suetonius Paulinus was appointed Governor
of Britain. He had orders to crush all resistance to Roman
rule. He believed that the island of Mona, off the Welsh
coast, was at the heart of the British and Celtic resistance,
as it was the home of the Druids – high-ranking, powerful
people in the Celtic culture who acted as judges and

religious leaders. They had been joined on Mona by warriors from different parts of Britain.

In 61 CE, Suetonius took a division of the Roman army to north Wales to wipe out the British rebel opposition.

Warrior Queen is set just as those Roman soldiers begin to mass on the coast opposite Mona, preparing to attack the British encampment.

After the story

According to Roman historians, 80 000 Britons died in the battle between Boudicca's forces and Suetonius's troops, compared with 400 Romans. There are conflicting accounts of what happened to Boudicca: one story says she died during the battle, another says she died shortly afterwards.

Acting on his orders from Rome to make sure there were no further major uprisings in Britain, Suetonius sent his army around Britain, attacking towns and villages, and killing warrior Britons and their families on a large scale. But the new Roman Emperor Nero feared that this cruelty would only make the Britons more hostile to the Romans, so he ordered Suetonius back to Rome and replaced him with a different governor, who was not so harsh a ruler.

Over time, although there were minor uprisings by some Britons, things settled down and Britain became Romanized.

When the Roman Empire began to collapse in the early fifth century CE, the official Roman army was withdrawn back to Rome. But most of the former soldiers stayed behind, as they had homes and families in the country.

Their descendants still live in Britain today.